Through Deep Waters

Finding Healing and Hope
in Devastating Grief

Michelle

Fitzpatrick Thomas

Published by Michelle Thomas

Edited by Jane Kesler

Cover photo by Jordan McQueen: (https://stocksnap.io/author/653)

ISBN e-book: 978-0-9911291-6-4

ISBN paperback: 978-0991129140

To purchase this book for trade
distribution, go to Amazon.com.

To contact the publisher, go to
www.KingdomCrossing.com.

201905V1

When I walk *through deep waters*
I know that You will be with me.

Kari Jobe

This book is dedicated to my dad—my first love, my rock, my counselor, my pastor, and my friend.

Contents

Foreword

This book is the account of one family's experience of sudden, tragic loss and grief, caused by a person addicted to drugs and alcohol—someone so impaired that he didn't even realize he had killed a person. This is also the story of thousands of families who suffer such tragic, preventable loss every year.

I have worked with many grieving people in my counseling practice over the last 30 years—people much like the ones in this story. It is my hope and prayer that the faith of this family and the resources shared here may be an inspiration and source of help to others in similar circumstances.

This book by my niece, Michelle Fitzpatrick Thomas, is a testimony to the enduring legacy of love that God poured out on her family. It is a testament to a love that cannot be broken by loss and grief; to a faith that transcends sorrow and pain; and to hope that sustains us in that faith.

Blessings,

Rev. Dr. John K. Hill, LMFT,

Approved Supervisor, AAMFT

Introduction

Grief is universal. If we live long enough, we all experience the loss of loved ones to death. This book tells my story of loss under senselessly tragic and criminal circumstances. I will deal with grief in general, offering helpful resources and encouragement for anyone struggling with the loss of a loved one, but I will also address grief resulting from the homicide of a loved one and other sudden tragic losses.

Losing a loved one when someone else is at fault is a different kind of grief than the loss of a loved one to cancer or a heart attack or even an accident. With a homicide, there are additional layers of complexity to deal with, involving all of the ins and outs of the legal process, emotional healing related to the actual crime, and forgiving the perpetrator and others who might have been involved.

Kenneth Doka explains in *Living with Grief after Sudden Loss*, "Sudden loss, death without forewarning, understandably creates special problems for survivors. Three of the most common include intensified grief, the shattering of a person's normal world and the existence of a series of concurrent crises and secondary losses."

Doka continues, "Grief is often intensified since there is little or no opportunity to prepare for the loss, say good-bye or finish unfinished business. In addition, the nature of the loss can bring on grief reactions such as anger, guilt and hopelessness, among others. There can also be a lingering sense of disorganization and consuming obsession with the person who died.

"Survivors of this kind of loss often experience a heightened sense of vulnerability and anxiety. Nothing appears safe anymore. Activities previously casually undertaken, such as driving a car, now can seem fraught with danger. Survivors may have to deal with pressures of media interest and intrusion, and of police or legal entanglements. They may experience secondary losses, too, like lost income or even their homes, and their inevitable search for the meaning of the loss can challenge spiritual resources." [1]

These words very accurately describe my life and how my loved ones have felt since experiencing our tragedy in 2015. Sometimes it helps us to heal when we write and talk about our experiences. That's one reason I'm sharing my journey here—I needed to work through all of the thoughts and emotions involved in my grief process, and it helped me to write it all down. Also, the Bible tells us in 2 Corinthians 1:4-5, "Praise be to the God and Father of our Lord Jesus Christ, the Father of compassion and the God of all comfort, who comforts us in all our troubles, so that we can comfort those in any trouble with the comfort we ourselves have received from God." My hope and prayer in sharing my story of tragedy and pain and forgiveness and healing is that

---

[1] Doka, Kenneth J., Ed. "Commentary." *Living with Grief after Sudden Loss*. Washington: The Hospice Foundation of America. 1996. Page 11. Print.

these words will be a salve to the souls of many who are suffering with the heartache of losing a loved one.

Grief is an interesting process. Because this world was created in perfection, we humans weren't designed to suffer the loss of loved ones. When sin entered history, we suddenly had to deal with an inexplicably ugly thing: grief. Grief isn't natural to us. It wasn't here from the beginning. We experience grief because we live in a sinful, broken world.

Our only hope in dealing with heart-wrenching grief is knowing that this world is not our home. When we belong to Christ, we look forward to an eternity free from heartache and pain and tears. We have the promise of re-uniting with our loved ones who have left this world before us.

So as you read my story, I hope you will relate to some of my raw emotions and experiences. I hope you will take comfort in some of the revelations that I have found through this grief process, and most of all, I hope you will draw closer to the Lord on your grief journey, as I have. He is my all in all and my everything. He carries me through each day, provides for my needs, and heals my broken heart. I eagerly await the day that I leave this broken world to spend eternity in His presence.

Chapter 1: Background

"But from everlasting to everlasting the Lord's love is with those who fear him, and his righteousness with their children's children." Psalm 103:17

I've heard it said that I come from "good stock." In agricultural terms, that means quality animals. In humans, I suppose that translates to good, hard-working, moral people.

My dad's dad was a public school teacher for many years. Dad's mom stayed home (as did most moms in those days) and, among many other things, raised five wonderful children. They have lived in the same community since 1951 when my dad, their first child, was an infant. My granddad went on to become the superintendent of schools in their county, where he served twelve years. Then upon retirement from the public school system, he worked for the Georgia Department of Education for another ten years. My grandfather passed away in 2017, and the next year the Georgia Legislature voted to name an intersection in his town after him. To say that my grandparents are well respected in their community is a bit of an understatement. They are pillars of the community, and I'm blessed to be their granddaughter.

My mom's parents were missionaries, so my mom grew up in Nigeria, West Africa. Missionary life presents a myriad of challenges, but my mom speaks quite fondly of her time in Africa, and she considered that "home" for years after they moved back to the U.S. to stay.

Mom's parents have both gone to Heaven now, but they were amazing and inspiring people. My granddad was brilliant; he had two doctoral degrees, played several instruments, and taught in various seminaries and colleges. My grandmother was a gifted teacher and artist. I have several of her charcoal masterpieces hanging in my house today.

After their first year of college, my parents married in 1969; both were 18. They had my older brother a couple of years later. I was born next. Three years later my best friend Suzanne was born, and then our younger brother three years after her.

When I was in elementary school, my dad worked hard and finished his bachelor's degree and went on to obtain a master's degree in counseling. He became a pastor when I was ten. He was a middle school teacher for several years and was a counselor and pastor for many years.

When I was in high school, my mom went back to college, while working full time and raising four kids, to finish her degree. In fact, when I started college, my older brother and Mom were also college students. Mom got her bachelor's degree when I was nineteen and had a successful career in human resources management. I'm very proud of her.

I graduated from college at 21 and started working as a medical social worker through a local home health agency. I made home visits to patients in five counties across Northeast Georgia, helping to connect them with services that they needed, praying with them during difficulties, and getting to know many of them like family.

The long car rides alone around beautiful Northeast Georgia gave me time to think and pray and hear from the Lord, and the experiences with those precious people changed me for the better. I will treasure the memories always, and I see now that God was teaching me how to help people, especially elderly people, deal with loss and grief in these experiences. So many of the patients with whom I worked had been married for several decades, and as they faced the loss of their lifelong partners, the grief was deep and raw and excruciating.

During these years, I began to long for my soul mate. I knew in my spirit that the Lord had someone in mind for me; I just couldn't understand why He was taking so long to bring him to me. I was 23 at the time, and people were beginning to wonder why I wasn't married yet. Even my sweet grandfather told me that maybe I was being too picky!

I knew that the second most important decision in my life was choosing the man I would marry. The first, of course, was my decision to follow Christ. I didn't want to make a mistake in such a monumental part of my life, for marrying the "wrong" person could prove to be disastrous, as it has for many, many people.

I pressed into the Lord, spent time memorizing Scripture, and asked God to make me into the wife that He wanted me to be for my future husband. I prayed for that man, whoever he was, and I tried to trust patiently for the Lord to bring us together.

God was good and faithful. A few months after I got serious about praying for and preparing myself for my future husband, God brought him into my life. We had mutual friends who introduced us. We had a short, whirlwind engagement, and we

married in early 1998, seven months after
we met.

Trevor and I have a financial story that we
told in another book, *Debt-Free Living in a
Debt-Filled World*. In a nutshell, after two
years of doing social work and shortly
before Trevor and I married, I took a job
at Christian Financial Concepts (now
Crown Financial Ministries). There I
learned God's principles for handling
money. I became passionate about
handling money God's way and sharing
what I learned with others.

When Trevor and I got married, our
finances were in very poor shape and we
had no assets to speak of. God directed us
to get out of debt and never borrow
money again, for anything. Over the
course of several years, we built our home
debt free by paying for it as we saved the
money.

About halfway through the building
process, almost four years into our
marriage, we found out we were expecting
our first baby, Caleb. Then about every

two years after Caleb was born, we added another baby, until we felt our quiver was full with four little blessings.

I started working from home when our first baby was born. I did that for several years until my load with homeschooling and keeping up with the house and activities became more than full time. My husband Trevor teaches mathematics at a local high school.

I was the first child in my family to get married. My older brother married shortly after me, then my sister about four years later, and our younger brother followed suit the year after that. Between the four marriages, we have eleven children. We all live within a few hours of each other, and we are a close, loving family. We enjoy gatherings and keeping up with family news and such.

My older brother and his wife are both teachers at a large Christian school. My sister is an RN and a lactation consultant at our local hospital, as well as a homeschooling mom. Her husband owns a video production company and is an amazing videographer. My younger brother is a marketing executive for a large company, and his wife is a talented editor and homeschooling mom.

Here's my point with all of the background that I just gave you: We are what most would consider "good people." We all have jobs. We pay taxes. We treat people well. We are generous. We are Christians.

There had always been what I imagined to be an invisible "umbrella" over my dad's family, protecting us from danger and sickness and significant family troubles and so forth. There had been no major illnesses; no deaths; not even any divorces among my grandparents, their five children and five in-laws, many grandchildren and grandchildren-in-law, and great-grandchildren. We could never have imagined or been prepared for what was in store for us. Homicide is no respecter of persons or families.

Chapter 2: May 4, 2015

"I have told you these things, so that in me you may have peace. In this world you will have trouble. But take heart! I have overcome the world." John 16:33

On Monday, May 4, 2015, I was enjoying a beautiful homeschool day with my four children and my nine-year-old niece. The girls had spent a couple of hours in the back yard building houses from sticks, berries, acorns, leaves, and such. Around 1:45 in the afternoon, I took pictures of their creations and shared them on my Facebook wall.

Before I closed Facebook, I saw an urgent post from one of my friends that went something like this:

"Please pray!!!! I just witnessed a bicyclist hit by a truck in Braselton. The truck left the scene, and the bicyclist is unresponsive."

My heart started pounding. You see, my dad lives in Braselton and in recent years, he had taken up cycling for recreation and exercise. I immediately feared the worst.

I tried several times to call my friend who witnessed the accident, but she didn't answer. I tried to call my dad multiple times. No answer. I called my sister, who lives close to my parents. No answer. I then called my mom at work and asked her if my dad was riding right then. He was. I told Mom about the post on Facebook and said that I would keep trying to reach my friend who had witnessed the crash. I called my husband and asked him to pray.

In the meantime, I rushed downstairs and told the kids to get in the car. I told them that someone had been hit riding their bike, and I wasn't sure if it was Papa or not. When I was about to walk out the door, my friend called. Sobbing, I asked her if it was my dad. She told me she didn't see his face, so she didn't know. She tried to assure me that lots of people ride bicycles around Braselton, and Braselton is a really big place. She said that it happened on the Oakwood side of Hwy 53 in

Braselton, hoping, I suppose, that he didn't ride in that area, and I told her that my dad lives around there. She said they were doing CPR on the man. She said she had described my dad to the investigator after she listened to the voicemail I had left her and asked him to call her if that matched the victim. He hadn't yet called, so she thought that was good news. She then prayed with me and for me and for the bicyclist, asking God to breathe His breath of life into him.

My dad wore a GPS tracker when he rode, so I called my mom back and asked if Dad's ride was still going. She checked it, and it had stopped—on Hwy. 53. So Mom left work immediately and rushed to find where he had stopped riding.

I had a forty-five-minute ride down to Braselton. While I was driving, I called my sister. Her husband went to check things out. A little while later, I called my sister back to see if Mark had found anything. While we were talking, he beeped in, so she switched to his call. When he hung up and her phone came back to my call, I heard the worst screams and sobs I could ever have imagined. I hung up immediately, knowing that my dad was dead.

My focus then was on getting the five children in my car safely to my parents' house. I feared that I would faint on the way, so I tried to keep my emotions in check. My mind was reeling. The kids kept asking if I knew anything yet, but I told them that we just needed to get to Mimi and Papa's house.

When we pulled into the driveway, my mom had just arrived from the scene of the crash. She opened the front door, and we held each other and sobbed. I told my kids that Papa had been killed, and we all held each other and cried for what seemed like forever. My husband came in from the crash scene, sobbing. My sister came in a few minutes later, and then her husband. We all sobbed while my mom called my two brothers to tell them the news.

A little while later, the coroner and a sheriff's deputy came to ask some questions. They told us that they had the driver in custody. I walked out with the deputy to get my dad's cycling shoes and sunglasses. I clung to the shoes and sobbed.

Anguish was the word of the day.

My dad was 64, in great health, with a wife of almost forty-six years, four kids, eleven grandkids, his parents, four siblings, brothers- and sisters-in-law, countless nieces, nephews, cousins, ten middle school students that he taught, multitudes of church friends, and on and on and on.

People started coming in that afternoon—church friends, aunts, uncles, my grandparents, cousins. It was the most surreal and unimaginably horrible day of my life.

That night, I hardly slept. I would doze and then immediately wake up, hoping desperately to be having a nightmare. I was devastated each time to realize that the nightmare was real.

The next few days, we spent a lot of time at my mom's house, hugging, crying, and talking. We had to wait until my dad was released from the GBI crime lab before we could make arrangements at the funeral home, but we began to plan his funeral. Heart-wrenching doesn't come close to describing this time.

We found out that the driver was charged with multiple counts, including DUI, first degree vehicular homicide, leaving the scene of an accident with death, open container, failure to maintain lane, failure to leave a safe distance, and improperly transferred license plate.

What do we do with that? To lose my dad suddenly was bad enough, but to lose him at the hands of someone who took substances into his body and chose to get behind the wheel of a vehicle multiplies the layers of tragedy in this whole situation. Someone was responsible for taking away my dad. In addition to all of the things that go along with losing a loved one, we were then dealing with state patrol investigators and district attorneys and a likely trial and sentencing. I felt as if I had been robbed.

I'm sure that many of you have had to say "goodbye" to someone precious to you. Although I always felt sympathy for others who were grieving the loss of a loved one, I couldn't truly understand their pain. I had never experienced anything like this before. I had lost a couple of good friends and had miscarried a baby, but that was the extent of my grieving. Nothing could have prepared me for this.

I know that I'm biased, but my dad was the best dad I could ever have hoped for. He was the most amazing Papa to his grandchildren. They adored him, and the feeling was mutual. It was evident to everyone who knew him.

My dad was my pastor. He was my counselor. He was my oldest child's middle school teacher. He was my occasional babysitter. He was my theology "professor." He was my go-to guy for technology questions or issues. I would call and chat with him while I was taking

walks in the evenings in my neighborhood.
He was my blog post proofreader. He was
my biggest cheerleader. He was one of my
very closest friends.

He was my rock.

My dad kept my sister's kids while she
worked as an RN. My older brother called
him after every UGA touchdown and after
all of his sons' ballgames. My younger
brother rode bicycles with him. He and
my mom have had "dates" every Friday
night for many years. He paid all of their
bills online, took out their trash, and
handled house maintenance. He came to
karate tournaments and piano recitals and
baseball games and basketball games and
soccer games and plays.

He was there for all of us. Always.

And now he's not. We all have a huge,
gaping, bleeding, festering hole in our lives
now.

In the first few days and weeks after my
dad was killed, I must have shed a million
tears. There will likely be many emotions

and many, many tears yet to come, but as strange as it sounds, I want to tell you that God is good, in spite of and even in the midst of this tragedy. He has already shown His goodness and mercy in many ways since my dad's death, that He's in control and He will take care of us. Here are a few examples:

A few days after my dad was killed, I called the witnesses who were listed on the crash report. I wanted to thank them personally for how they helped my dad and the role they played in assisting the authorities with apprehending the driver who killed him. After talking with one witness and hearing his story, I learned that he was a pastor. Another witness, who administered CPR to my dad, was such a sweet Christian young man. He was with my dad when he left this world and entered the presence of Jesus. I mentioned above that one of my friends, a precious sister in the Lord, witnessed the crash as well. I'll always be thankful that my dad was surrounded by fellow believers when he took his last breath here on earth.

I mentioned that my dad taught at our homeschool academy, so we needed to find someone to replace him, and soon. I knew that we could find someone to teach, but I was so sad that the middle school kids would be missing out on the pastor's heart that Dad brought to his students. Do you know who God sent, almost immediately after Dad's death? Two people: A pastor friend to teach our Bible classes and Dad's brother, another "Mr. Fitz," a long-time middle school teacher and then elementary school principal, to teach math and science. Even in this incredible tragedy, God showed us his faithfulness and goodness.

Dad's funeral was a beautiful celebration of not only his life but of the goodness and mercy of God. We have heard many stories of people who were touched and changed by being in the service that day.

God has opened many doors for our family to tell others about Him through this tragedy. We made many calls to cancel services or subscriptions or to get help with billing questions as my mom tried to work through all of the legal and business issues she was left with. Over and over again, as we explained what happened, we were able to share that God is with us and is taking care of us. He will not let this tragedy go to waste. He will continue to use it to further His purposes and to touch lives for His Kingdom.

So in the days following the crash, even though my heart was shattered into pieces, I chose to trust in my "Abba Father," my Heavenly Daddy, to fill the holes and to carry me through this life. Although right now it seems like forever until I will see my Dad again, I know that in God's timing it's only the blink of an eye and we will be reunited.

I've always been afraid of dying and leaving this world. It's natural to fear the unknown, but I'm no longer afraid, because I know that my Dad is there waiting for me. I'm eager to join him there, to worship my Awesome God for ever and ever.

This pain and heartache were not in God's plan for us. Because of sin, we live in a broken world and we all suffer, but soon God will send Jesus for us, the church, His Bride, and we will be with Him for eternity. Everything will be made right.

A picture of my parents, taken the Christmas before Dad was killed.

"He will wipe every tear from their eyes. There will be no more death or mourning or crying or pain, for the old order of things has passed away." (Revelation 21:4)

As I've never prayed before, I say, "Come, Lord Jesus!"

Chapter 3: My "Crash" Course in Grief

"The Lord himself goes before you and will be with you; he will never leave you nor forsake you. Do not be afraid; do not be discouraged." Deuteronomy 31:8

A 1989 study "found that 23% of family members murdered or killed by a drunk driver developed post-traumatic stress disorder at some point after the death. Interestingly, very few differences were noted between the two victim populations, thus destroying the myth that crashes are mere 'accidents' that should not result in as much trauma for family members as murders or other homicides." Janice Lord goes on to explain that murders often involve some degree of psychological preparation because the victim might have been stalked, experienced previous assault by the murderer, or been involved in dangerous activities that could lead to death, like drugs or gangs. However, "vehicular crashes are among the most unanticipated of deaths."[2]

Ms. Lord continues, "We tend to think of intentional murders when we hear the words 'violent death.' However, the extremely severe trauma experienced in vehicular crashes—so severe that it caused death—becomes a crucial component of bereavement counseling."[3]

This has been a significant hurdle in my grief journey. Ms. Lord explains that "the suddenness component, coupled with lack of closure, often leads survivors to feel driven to go immediately to the body of their loved one, regardless of its condition." [4] My husband, my sister's husband, and my mom all rushed to the scene of the crash, but police officers wouldn't let them near my dad.

---

[2] Lord, Janice H. "America's Number One Killer: Vehicular Crashes" *Living with Grief After Sudden Loss*. Washington: The Hospice Foundation of America. 1996. Pages 25-26, 29. Print.
[3] Ibid
[4] Ibid

I did see my dad briefly at the church, just before they closed his casket for the funeral, and he did not look at all like himself. The mortician must have had a difficult job in making him appear presentable, because his injuries were quite extensive. I have replayed what I imagined the crash to be like over and over in my mind through the years. It would be fair to say that the scene (imagined, though it is in my mind) has haunted me.

I know enough details from visiting the scene of the crash and from speaking with the state patrol officer and some of the witnesses to know that my dad died a terribly violent death. I know that I shouldn't dwell on such things, but it's very hard to keep my mind from going there. When I sink into that awful train of thought, I have to pull myself out of it quickly by thinking about other things. It's been helpful to have my kids around, because they keep things upbeat and are a distraction when I'm tempted to sink into the mire of the tragedy.

As I have prayed through this aspect of my grief journey, I have asked the Lord to bring healing to my mind regarding the details of the crash. I know that Satan wants me to dwell on the horror of it, but God wants to bring healing and restoration and peace. If you are struggling with imagining the details of your loved one's death, I encourage you to make it a matter of much prayer. The Lord does not want us to dwell on the trauma that we have experienced and let it sour other parts of our lives.

In the days and weeks after Dad was killed, I wondered if there would ever come a time when I didn't think about him every waking moment of every day. One of my friends, whose father was killed in a mining accident years ago, assured me that the day would come when I wouldn't dwell on his death each moment. Thankfully, she was right, and I'm able to function better now.

The months following the crash were, hands down, the hardest of my entire life. I cried daily for the first several months straight, and even now, several years later, tears will erupt when I least expect it. I try to keep the tears inside until I'm alone at night…often in the shower. There the tears can flow and I can pour out my hurts and heartache to God without upsetting anyone else. Sometimes, out of the blue it hits me that Dad is really gone, and it feels like I've been punched in the stomach.

I want to discuss some of the things that I learned about grief in the few months immediately following the crash….the good, the bad, and the ugly. And believe me, parts of it are ugly.

The "experts" say that there are stages of grief, such as denial, anger, bargaining, depression, and acceptance. I can't point to specific stages that I've been through; maybe that will come in time. I just know that it hurts. And it's messy. And I've run the gamut of emotions from one day to another or even from one moment to another.

As my mom and I were sitting by Dad's fresh grave one day, an older lady stopped by the cemetery to put flowers on a grave that I assume belonged to her husband. Her less than comforting words were this, "Honey, it doesn't ever get any easier."

But what about "Time heals all wounds."

and

"Weeping may remain for a night, but rejoicing comes in the morning." (Psalm 30:5)

and

"A time to weep and a time to laugh, a time to mourn and a time to dance." (Ecclesiastes 3:4)?

Where's the hope that this pain won't last forever?

Elisabeth Kübler-Ross and David Kessler have this to say: "The reality is that you will grieve forever. You will not 'get over' the loss of a loved one; you will learn to live with it. You will heal and you will rebuild yourself around the loss you have suffered. You will be whole again but you

Michelle Fitzpatrick Thomas

will never be the same. Nor should you be the same, nor would you want to"[5]

Going back to our homeschool academy a couple of months after Dad was killed was excruciating for me. Dad was one of our middle school teachers, and I was the school administrator at the time. I spent well over 600 hours with Dad at school in his last year of life. When I was there, I could almost hear his voice coming from his classroom across the hall from my office. I could almost see him walking down the hall in his slow, confident gait. I could almost smell his cologne on my children's clothes, because they would greet him with a hug each morning at the beginning of school. Thankfully, I had the summer after he was killed to work through some of the emotions before I had to go back for a new school year, and I tried to put on my "happy face" every

---

[5] Kübler-Ross, Elisabeth and Kessler, David. *On Grief and Grieving: Finding the Meaning of Grief Through the Five Stages of Loss.* New York: Scribner. 2014. Web.

day at school, but it was still very difficult even to look in his classroom.

Early on, anger was a prominent feeling for me. I wouldn't say that I was stuck in the anger "phase" of grief, but I experienced angry moments off and on, out of the blue, for no apparent reason. I screamed at God for taking my dad away. I screamed at the man who killed him (well, not really "at" him, but in the privacy of my home). I was mad at Dad for riding on a busy road. I was less than patient with my children at times, because it was hard to keep the anger from flowing out. I had little patience with senseless quarrels and the insignificant squabbles of others. It was as if I had crossed over a line. I could then see what was truly important in life, and I didn't want to spend my time and energy on trivial issues that have no eternal value.

I read a book called *Forgiving the Unforgivable*. The author lost his father, grandmother, and great-grandmother to a drunk driver over 20 years ago, and he discusses the process of forgiving someone for something that caused so much pain. He says that it took him a long time (years) to come to the place where he could forgive the driver. In fact, for some time, he wanted the driver to die for what he had done.

I will discuss forgiveness more in a later chapter, but to say that I've forgiven the driver who killed my dad would be true and false. When he comes to mind, I have to make a conscious choice to forgive him, over and over again. I think it's a process that we have to go through, of releasing the perpetrator in our minds and praying for him or her until we finally feel no ill will toward the person.

I do pray for the man who killed Dad—I pray for him often. I pray that he will come to know the Lord through this tragedy. If this makes any sense, I don't want my dad's death to be wasted; I want Dad's life and death to lead his killer to Christ. I know without a shadow of a doubt that if Dad had been given the choice to die so that his killer would gain eternal life, he would've willingly given his life. (Who knows? Maybe Dad *was* given that choice in the instant before he was killed.) Wouldn't that be how God operates? To use something absolutely horrific to bring about something eternally awesome?!

Our family had a long road of difficulties concerning the legal aspect of Dad's death. I will give many details about this in a later chapter, but it took almost two years for the entire legal process to be resolved. Unfortunately, this kept the details of the crash and Dad's death in the forefront of our minds and we were forced to re-live the tragedy and loss over and over again through the legal process.

But here are some positives in this tragic journey:

One thing that I've experienced since Dad's death is a loss of fear. I'm no longer afraid of death and dying because my daddy has gone before me. It's comforting to know that He is in heaven holding the babies that my sister and I miscarried until we get there and can hold them ourselves.

He was an awesome Papa to his grandkids here on earth, and he's being an awesome Papa now to the three who are with him in heaven.

Another positive is that I've lost some of my shyness about talking to others concerning matters of faith. I've always been very reserved and almost afraid to talk to strangers, for fear of sounding dumb or coming across as odd. Since Dad's death, I have a new boldness and a desire to share with others what's truly important in life: a relationship with Jesus.

I often wonder if it's harder to lose a loved one instantly and tragically as we have or slowly and painfully, from a disease. I think to myself that I would give my right arm to be able to tell my dad goodbye, to give him one last hug and tell him how very much I love him. But if I had had to watch my big, strong, wise daddy waste away from a horrible disease or injury, I don't think I could have endured it. Even in tragedy, God is merciful and kind.

I've prayed for Jesus to come back for His church many, many times since Dad was killed. I'm ready to leave this earth; I'm ready for the pain and heartache to end. I wouldn't say that I was "depressed," but early on after the crash, I had a desire to die. In fact, several in our family have expressed these feelings, including some of our small children. Of course, I never thought of killing myself, but I would have been very happy for God to take me from this world at any time. My husband thought I was nuts and told me that I was being selfish and that he and our children would be devastated. That's true, I suppose, and I wouldn't wish that pain on them for anything....I just wanted to be with my daddy again, and I was tired of hurting. I couldn't imagine living 40 or 50 more years on this earth without him. I didn't see how I possibly could.

And then, there's this: "I can do everything through him who gives me strength." Philippians 4:13.

Do you see that?

I *can* because He *gives*.

If God wants me to live 50 more years here, I have to trust that He will give me the strength. If He wants to take me Home tomorrow, I have to trust that He will give my loved ones the strength to bear it. He is enough.

My aunt sent me a devotional that gave me peace and increased my longing to be Home. Here's an excerpt: "Think about the comfortable feeling you have as you open your front door [after a long trip]. That's but a hint of what we'll feel some day on arriving at the place our Father has lovingly and personally prepared for us in heaven. We will finally—and permanently—be 'at home' in a way that defies description." [6]

This world is not our Home. We are merely passing through. We are aliens and strangers on this earth. But our journey here needs to mean something. We have Kingdom work to do on our way through

---

[6] https://www.guideposts.org/inspiration/inspiring-quotes/heaven

this life, and I believe that Jesus won't be back for His church until we've finished the work He has given us.

Life is hard. In fact, it stinks sometimes. But God is good. He is faithful. He loves us. And He's coming for us soon.

I find now at four years after my dad was killed that the pain is still there and it is still intense at times, but God has done a lot of healing in my life as well. I am thankful that I'm not where I was right after the crash, and I would never want to go back to that fresh, raw, bitterly heartrending time.

I still find myself longing for heaven and missing my dad immensely, but I think that something is wrong if we, as believers, aren't longing for our heavenly home. What awaits us on the other side of this world is better than we can even imagine. For that, I am eternally thankful. In the words of Matt Maher…..

Because He lives, I can face tomorrow.

Because He lives, every fear is gone.

I know He holds my life, my future in His hands.[7]

My Dad

7

https://www.azlyrics.com/lyrics/mattmaher/becausehelivesamen.html

Chapter 4: The Legal Process

"Do not take revenge, my friends, but leave room for God's wrath, for it is written, 'It is mine to avenge; I will repay,' says the Lord." Romans 12:19

After Dad was killed, we did some internet searching and found that his killer has a very extensive criminal history from his home state of Indiana. Convictions included multiple drug charges and DUIs, dating back to the 1980s. He had even hit and injured someone while driving years ago, but no resolution to that case could be found. He was 51 when he killed my dad, so he had lived plenty long enough to get his act together and be more responsible.

At the time of the crash, the killer was already serving a twenty-year probation for multiple counts of felony "theft by deception," meaning he had defrauded several people by arranging to do roofing work for them, taking their money, and then never doing the work. He was on probation in the county where I live; the crash happened in a neighboring county where my parents' house was.

The day after the crash, the killer was released from jail on bond, in spite of the fact that he was on felony probation in the neighboring county. I still can't believe that in this technological age, our local justice system isn't equipped with an online database of offenders who are serving probation elsewhere and should be detained, if arrested.

Nevertheless, the killer was a free man. We feared that he would flee the area, but we were assured by law enforcement officials that he would stay put because he had multiple health issues and relied on the government assistance that he was receiving in our county to survive. I contacted the probation office to see what was being done to apprehend him. I was told by his probation officer that they had sworn out a warrant for his arrest. We waited and prayed that he would be found soon.

Every day for several weeks, I searched the local jail's website for the defendant's name, to see if he had been arrested. Then finally on June 9—ironically my dad's birthday—he was booked into the jail. We felt as though the Lord was giving us a gift in honor of my dad—his killer was behind bars and unable to harm anyone else.

A couple of months after the arrest, the probation officer called to let us know that the defendant would have a hearing regarding his probation violations. All of the charges surrounding the crash that killed my dad equated to violations of the terms of his probation. He had to either admit that he had violated his probation or deny it. The day of the hearing arrived in August. We were told that if the defendant admitted to the violations, one of us would be allowed to speak to the judge before he sentenced him by revoking part or all of the probation and sending him to prison. I had prepared some thoughts on behalf of our family, but the judge postponed the hearing until December, in the hopes that the criminal investigation of the crash by the Georgia State Patrol would be completed by then and he could make a better ruling.

So with a knot in our stomachs, we waited for the hearing, which was scheduled for December 29. Talk about a damper on the Christmas season. I had a constant nauseous feeling in my stomach during the weeks leading up to the hearing.

My sister and I met with the district attorney who would be presenting the evidence to the judge at the probation revocation hearing. He walked us through what would happen, and I discussed with him the victim impact statement that I would be delivering on behalf of our family.

The entire investigation of the crash wasn't completed until months after the probation revocation hearing, but a very important piece of evidence was released to the DA's office: the toxicology report showed that the defendant had *cocaine* and Xanax in his system when he killed my dad. This was a game changer for the defendant. He couldn't defend the fact that there was cocaine in his system. Instead of a hearing to determine the defendant's guilt or innocence in violating probation, we were told that he would admit to the probation violations and would be sentenced on December 29. We would have the opportunity to speak to the judge before he pronounced the sentence.

I have never been as nervous as I was the day of the sentencing. I had never been involved in a court hearing of any sort before, and here I was, being called as a witness to speak to a courtroom regarding my dad's death. I had agonized over my statement, sending multiple revisions to my siblings and mom and the DA's office to get their thoughts and input.

I felt literally sick the morning of the hearing. I sat down for a few moments to pray and seek the Lord through His Word for comfort and peace. I was overwhelmed with His goodness and love for us when my eyes "happened to land on" Psalm 94. It reads,

O LORD, the God who avenges,
O God who avenges, shine forth.
Rise up, O Judge of the earth; pay
back to the proud what they
deserve. How long will the wicked
be jubilant?

They pour out arrogant words; all
the evildoers are full of boasting.
They crush your people, O LORD;
they oppress your inheritance. They
slay the widow and the alien; they
murder the fatherless. They say,
"The LORD does not see; the God
of Jacob pays no heed."

Take heed, you senseless ones
among the people; you fools, when
will you become wise? Does he
who implanted the ear not hear?
Does he who formed the eye not
see? Does he who disciplines
nations not punish? Does he who
teaches man lack knowledge? The
LORD knows the thoughts of
man; he knows that they are futile.

Michelle Fitzpatrick Thomas

Blessed is the man you discipline,
O LORD, the man you teach from
your law; you grant him relief from
days of trouble, till a pit is dug for
the wicked. For the LORD will not
reject his people; he will never
forsake his inheritance. Judgment
will again be founded on
righteousness, and all the upright in
heart will follow it.

Who will rise up for me against the
wicked? Who will take a stand for
me against evildoers? Unless the
LORD had given me help, I would
soon have dwelt in the silence of
death. When I said, "My foot is
slipping," your love, O LORD,
supported me. When anxiety was
great within me, your consolation
brought joy to my soul.

Can a corrupt throne be allied with
you—one that brings on misery by
its decrees? They band together
against the righteous and condemn
the innocent to death. But the
LORD has become my fortress,

and my God the rock in whom I take refuge. He will repay them for their sins and destroy them for their wickedness; the LORD our God will destroy them.

Wow. I was blown away by the very personal way that the Lord answered my cries for help. The hearing was still horrible and nerve racking and was the hardest thing that I had ever had to do, but I was assured that the Lord was with me.

With shaking hands and tears streaming down my face, I read the following statement to the judge that day as the victim advocate sat beside me and held onto me to give support:

Your Honor, thank you for allowing me this opportunity to speak today. My name is Michelle Fitzpatrick Thomas. My dad was David Fitzpatrick, who was hit and killed on May 4th by [the defendant]. I brought some pictures of my dad and our family today so you can see who I will be describing. I would really like for [the defendant] to see these, as well.

On behalf of my mom, my sister and her husband, my brothers and their wives, my husband, my dad's parents, my dad's brothers and sisters, and other family and friends who are here today, I want to give you a glimpse of what [the defendant] took from us on May 4th.

My three siblings and I lost a dear friend, a mentor, a counselor, a sounding board, a babysitter, and an amazing dad. Our four spouses lost the most supportive and loving father-in-law anyone could ask for.

My siblings and I have 11 very heartbroken children, from 5 to 13 years old, who were robbed of the best Papa that any child could ever imagine. It is heart-wrenching to hold them while they cry themselves to sleep at night because they miss Papa so badly. My biggest fear is that they will grow up and forget him.

My grandparents had to watch their son be buried—something no parents should have to endure. My dad's two brothers and two sisters lost their older brother and dear friend.

And most heartbreaking is that my amazing mom lost her soul mate of 46 years. They married when they were 18 years old and have grown more in love with each passing year. She is learning to live alone for the first time in her life. There will be no more Friday night date nights, no more anniversary trips to St. Simons, no more memories made. And not only did she lose her best friend—but because [the defendant] didn't even have the minimum legally required auto insurance, she also lost thousands of dollars in funeral expenses along with my dad's income.

As a licensed professional counselor, my dad spent many years helping people in this community—people much like [the defendant]. He worked with those dealing with drug and alcohol addictions, families in crisis, and teens in trouble. He worked at Laurelwood [mental health hospital], helping people to find healing and hope in the midst of serious mental illnesses.

He worked for many years in private practice at The Family Project counseling center. And maybe most ironic is the time he spent working with prisoners at Lee Arrendale Correctional Institute, helping inmates in a residential treatment program to break free from their addictive behaviors so they would be ready to be productive citizens upon their release.

My dad's life was spent helping others. He was a pastor for 30 years, the last 17 of which were right around the corner at the Gainesville Vineyard Church. The church is still without a pastor since my dad's death. Dad made many trips to Peru, so even people on another continent are grieving over their lost missionary and friend.

And for the last two years, he taught the precious middle school students at our local homeschool academy (one of those students was my oldest child, who adored his Papa more than words can express). Those students were absolutely heartbroken to lose their wise and compassionate teacher so suddenly and tragically.

For several years, my dad had enjoyed his hobby and exercise of choice—cycling—and had logged thousands of hours on the roads. Cycling helped him to stay in great shape, with the intention of living many more years to enjoy his family and serve the Lord. He was extremely careful and considerate of motorists when he rode.

On May 4th, he was almost home from a 12-mile ride when [the defendant]—already on felony probation—made the **choice** to get high on cocaine and get behind the wheel, hit my dad, leaving him dead in a ditch, and flee the scene with no regard for his life, having to be chased down by witnesses so he could be arrested.

We understand that [the defendant] has a long criminal history. So what we struggle with is why? Why was he a free man on May 4th and allowed to kill my dad—a productive, respected, and loved member of society? Why was [the defendant] not behind bars already? My dad could've finished his ride with no complications, and our lives would've gone on as usual.

Instead, four days ago we went to the cemetery to wish my dad a Merry Christmas. Our lives have been turned upside down because of [the defendant's] criminal actions. Our family, the community, and the world have been robbed of an amazing man with an unbelievable heart for others. We ask for justice.

Nothing can bring back my dad, but we humbly ask that [the defendant] be given the maximum sentence possible today so he is not free to bring devastation like this on any other family ever again. I wouldn't wish this pain on my worst enemy.

Mr. [defendant], we pray for you— a lot. We want you to find healing and redemption through Jesus Christ. Jesus is the only hope that any of us has. We choose to forgive you for what you have done to us, and we want you to spend eternity with us—and with my dad—in

Heaven. Please open your heart to the Lord and ask Him to help you.

As I close, I want to share a verse from the Bible with you, Mr. [defendant]. The book of Isaiah, chapter 55, verses 6 and 7 say this, "Seek the Lord while he may be found; call on him while he is near. Let the wicked forsake his way and the evil man his thoughts. Let him turn to the Lord, and he will have mercy on him, and to our God, for **he** will freely pardon."

Thank you, Your Honor.

After my statement, the judge had some things to say. He looked back at the records from the 2010 trial and saw that—very unfortunately for us—the DA prosecuting that case had told him that she knew of no prior offenses and failed to provide him with any of the defendant's criminal history from the national database. So based on the erroneous knowledge that this was his first criminal offense and in the hopes that the defendant would work hard and pay back those he had robbed, the judge sentenced him in 2010 to twenty years of probation with no prison time.

Just five years later, when it's possible he would've still been in prison had the judge known about his criminal background and given him actual prison time, the defendant killed my dad.

The defendant had about fifteen years left on his twenty-year probation sentence when he killed my dad. We were praying that the judge would revoke the entire amount so he would serve the rest of his sentence in prison. We almost got what we wanted. The judge revoked twelve of the fifteen years. So a few weeks later, the defendant was sent to the state prison in Milledgeville, GA to serve 12 years for felony theft by deception and await the trial for killing my dad.

The wheels of justice move quite slowly here in Georgia. It took over a year for the Georgia State Patrol to complete their very thorough investigation of the crash and deliver it to the district attorney's office. The county in which my dad was killed holds court only three times each year. The docket stays fairly full, so we had to wait our turn for the case to come to trial.

After he had received the full investigation, the DA met with our family and discussed offering the defendant a plea deal. Because the killer had two prior felony convictions, he said that any sentence he received could be applied as what's called "recidivist," meaning that he will serve every day of his sentence and won't be eligible for parole. The DA felt that offering a sentence of twenty years, fifteen of which would be served, would be fair, so that is the plea deal that the DA offered. The defendant rejected the sentence. A counter-deal was offered of twelve years to serve, which was also rejected.

So twenty months after the crash, we were preparing for our case finally to go to trial. The thought of sitting through a trial with testimony about Dad's death, and viewing crime scene and autopsy photos made us physically ill, but we didn't want the killer to receive simply a slap on the hand and be out in society to kill again. If a trial is what it took to bring justice, that's what we were prepared to do.

A few weeks before the trial was to start, the DA called and said that the defense had offered a counter plea deal: a thirty-year sentence to serve fifteen, but the fifteen would be non-recidivist, which meant that he could be eligible for parole at some point.

We talked and prayed about this option and felt that it was a fair sentence, considering current Georgia law. So the defendant was officially sentenced to thirty years—fifteen to serve in prison and the subsequent fifteen to serve on probation. We plan to be involved in the parole process and do all we can to convince the parole board to keep the killer behind bars for the entire fifteen years. Given his criminal history and obvious disregard for the law, he will likely be a danger to society even after spending many years in prison.

Homicide is defined as "the killing of one human being by another." In the case of vehicular homicide, the *Merriam-Webster* online dictionary says, "homicide committed by the use of a vehicle (as an automobile or boat)."[8]

The legal consequences for intentional homicide (murder) are usually much greater than those for "unintentional" homicides like our case. However, I would argue that when a person *intentionally* introduces intoxicating substances into his or her body and then *chooses* to get behind the wheel of a 2,000-pound "weapon," killing a person is a likely outcome and therefore should be prosecuted more severely. Unfortunately, the law looks at it differently.

Here are some things that I learned through the gut-wrenching legal process surrounding my dad's death.

Justice through the legal system does nothing to heal our broken hearts. It

---

[8] https://www.merriam-webster.com/dictionary/homicide#legalDictionary

brings me no joy to know that Dad's killer is behind bars for many years. I would much rather have my dad back here with me and the man who killed him living a productive life in society.

There are many precious, compassionate people who work in the criminal justice system, but nevertheless, it is a badly flawed system. One mistake can prove to be fatal. If the DA in 2010 had done her job, my dad might still be alive. Also, countless offenders get simply a slap on the wrist for drug and alcohol offenses because the jails are overcrowded and there aren't enough effective treatment programs in place to help them find true healing for their addictions. This means that there are multitudes of people out in society at any given time who are wrestling with addictions to drugs and alcohol and who might be a danger to others.

It's wise to stay informed and keep in contact with the authorities during each step of the legal process. Victims and families can fall through the cracks unless they remain diligent.

Facing Dad's killer was extremely difficult. I was almost paralyzed, knowing that the man sitting across from me took my dad's life and showed no remorse. What I keep trying to come back to is that *he needs Jesus*.

It's essential to pray, pray, and pray some more, even when you don't feel like it. Remember that your situation and mine didn't catch God off guard. He still has a plan for us and has promised to care for us. He has shown us His provision and compassion and love each step of this very painful and difficult process, and He will do the same for you. He works in us and through us as we seek Him day by day and moment by moment.

Like it or not, being the victims of a publicized tragedy brought attention. People knew that my dad was a pastor and that we are a Christian family, so they watched us to see how we would respond. We tried to honor Christ in all of our actions and in the midst of our brokenness. That's what Dad would have wanted.

If you're dealing with the legal system regarding the loss of a loved one, I encourage you to reach out to the victim advocate in your county for information and support. He or she is there to help you through the very difficult process that is before you. In our area, that person is part of the county district attorney's office.

It was overwhelming when we found ourselves thrown into the legal system after losing a loved one in a criminal act. Our heads were already in a fog from the grief, and we were suddenly bombarded by an overload of information and terminology that was virtually foreign to us. I encourage you to lean on those who are there to help you: the investigators, the district attorney's office, and any others who specialize in victim services in your area.

By default, I became the point person for our family and was the one who communicated with the district attorneys' offices, probation officers, and the media. I gathered information and then kept all of the immediate and extended family members informed of the legal proceedings and news. I think for me this was a way to cope with the trauma in the short-term. I felt like if I stayed actively involved in the process, I was somehow helping my dad. That was just one of the many irrational things that victims think during times of emotional trauma, but it helped me to remain busy in this way.

If you have the opportunity to stay involved in the legal process concerning your loved one's case, you might find that it is a healing thing for you, too. If it is more stressful and difficult than it is helpful, then by all means let someone else take over that role.

Chapter 5: Forgiveness

"Be kind and compassionate to one another, forgiving each other, just as in Christ God forgave you."
Ephesians 4:32

"Most people are generally angry that with all of our scientific achievements, we have not found cures for AIDS, cancer, leukemia or the myriad of other terminal illnesses that plague us. However, a vehicular crash [and any other type of homicide] is *somebody's fault*. While the specific victim was not preselected and run down, the offender was usually negligent through intoxication, speed, lack of attentiveness, allowing exhaustion to set in, etc. Therefore, the crash could so easily have been prevented." [9] This fact makes the grieving process quite complicated.

---

[9] Lord, Janice H. "America's Number One Killer: Vehicular Crashes." *Living with Grief After Sudden Loss*. Washington: The Hospice Foundation of America. 1996. Page 32. Print.

Immediately after the crash, I felt great compassion for the driver of the vehicle that hit and killed my dad. I didn't know much about the circumstances of the crash yet. I didn't know the driver was intoxicated. I didn't know about his long criminal history. I just assumed that it was a terrible accident—maybe the driver had looked down at his phone for a moment, or perhaps something had caused him to swerve and he lost control— regardless, I knew that what just happened would ruin the driver's life just like it had ours.

The sheriff's deputy and coroner came to bring Dad's belongings a few hours after the crash and told us that they had caught the perpetrator and they were sure they had the right person in custody. (An interesting little side note: the deputy gave us Dad's iPhone that he had with him when he was hit. Though Dad was killed, there wasn't a scratch on his phone. I believe this would have made him very happy, because he was quite the techie and loved his gadgets!) The deputy didn't give us many details; I'm not sure we could have absorbed them, anyway. We were all in complete shock, but still I remember feeling sorry for the driver.

My compassion melted away the day after the crash, when I began to read local news articles stating that the man who killed Dad had been charged with DUI and driving with an open container, as well as multiple other charges (seventeen in total), including hit-and-run, reckless driving, and improperly registered license plate. That's how we found out that this wasn't just an "accident."

Rage welled up in me.

To add to the depth of our tragedy, we discovered just weeks after the crash that the driver's car insurance had been cancelled three months prior to the crash, so he had absolutely no way to compensate my mother for all that he had stolen from her. She had to foot the bill for the funeral expenses; she lost my dad's income; she lost her protector; she lost her soul mate.

As a believer, I know that I have to forgive others when they sin against me. We are told in Mark 11:25, "And when you stand praying, if you hold anything against anyone, forgive them, so that your Father in heaven may forgive you your sins." I am certainly in need of God's forgiveness, so it's essential that I forgive others. I know those things in my head; applying them in a situation like this is a different matter entirely.

I'm a fairly reserved person. I would never dream of fussing at a stranger or causing a scene in public. But alone in my own house, I screamed at the man who killed my dad. I was so angry at him for his horrible, selfish, reckless actions that took away my rock, my counselor, my friend, my mom's soul mate, and my kids' Papa.

I didn't reserve all of my anger for the perpetrator. I also let God have it. I screamed at Him. I asked him "why" more times than I can count. I pleaded with Him to take me, too, because the pain felt unbearable.

Years ago, I heard a sermon about forgiveness, and it was described as a process. Each time the offense comes to mind, it's important to *choose* to forgive that person for what he or she did. Over time as we choose to forgive and release the perpetrator into God's hands, it becomes easier and easier to forgive.

Forgiveness is important, not for the person who offended or harmed us, but for our own spiritual wellbeing. When we carry around the offense for months or years at a time, it affects us. We become bitter, sour people, and often our bodies suffer physical consequences as well. It's important to work through the process of forgiving so that God can bring healing and restoration to our lives in His timing.

If you're struggling with forgiving the person who took your loved one's life, I encourage you to meditate on the following verses, praying through each one until you feel peace from the Lord.

Matthew 26:28:

"This is my blood of the covenant, which is poured out for many for the forgiveness of sins."

Matthew 6:9-15:

"This, then, is how you should pray:

'Our Father in heaven, hallowed be your name, your kingdom come, your will be done on earth as it is in heaven. Give us today our daily bread. Forgive us our debts, as we also have forgiven our debtors. And lead us not into temptation. but deliver us from the evil one.'

For if you forgive men when they sin against you, your heavenly Father will also forgive you. But if you do not forgive men their sins, your Father will not forgive your sins."

Micah 7:18-19:

"Who is a God like you, who pardons sin and forgives the transgression of the remnant of his inheritance? You do not stay angry forever but delight to show mercy. You will again have compassion on us; you will tread our sins underfoot and hurl all our iniquities into the depths of the sea."

Isaiah 1:18:

"'Come now, let us reason together,' says the Lord. 'Though your sins are like scarlet, they shall be as white as snow; though they are red as crimson, they shall be like wool.'"

Daniel 9:9:

"The Lord our God is merciful and forgiving, even though we have rebelled against him."

God tells us in Hebrews 10:17 that He will remember our sins no more. But as humans, we remember when people hurt us. We have to wrestle with the human desire for revenge. We have to choose moment by moment to release the perpetrator to the Lord by forgiving him.

It might be encouraging to you that, "In a study of 184 family members of someone killed in a drunk-driving crash, Dr.

Dorothy Mercer (1991) found that those reporting having had a lot or some faith before the sudden death of their loved one found their faith strengthened by the crisis they had endured. Those having little or no faith prior to the killing of their loved one found their faith staying the same or weakening. Overall, nearly three times as many claimed their faith was strengthened as was weakened as a result of the crash."[10] God uses all things in our lives to mold us and shape us into what He wants us to be. As unpleasant as it is, your grief is part of that process.

Be aware that coming to the point of fully forgiving the perpetrator and feeling emotionally healthy again might take a very long time. "Most research about anticipatory grieving and death following long illness or injury tells us that the expected recovery period ranges from two to four years, based on numerous

---

[10] Lord, Janice H. "America's Number One Killer: Vehicular Crashes." *Living with Grief After Sudden Loss*. Washington: The Hospice Foundation of America. Page 35. Print.

variables. Research about sudden, violent death tells us to expect a four-to-seven-year recovery period, acknowledging that recovery is never complete. (Lehman & Wortman, 1987; Mercer, 1993). Many have found that the pain of mourning increases during the second and third years (Rinear, 1988; Ditchick, 1990), possibly because much of the first year is spent psychologically numbed to the reality of what happened." [11]

So give yourself the time that you need to work through the raw emotions and feelings involved in your grief process. Be patient with yourself. Surround yourself with people who will support you through the process, rather than those who might rush you to "get over it." Your grief is your own, and no one, except God, can truly know how you feel and how long it will take for you to be healthy again. He

---

[11] Lord, Janice H. "America's Number One Killer: Vehicular Crashes." *Living with Grief After Sudden Loss*. Washington: The Hospice Foundation of America. 1996. Page 36. Print.

will walk with you all the way and heal
your broken heart.

Chapter 6: Substance Abuse

"Everything is permissible'—but not everything is beneficial. 'Everything is permissible'—but not everything is constructive. Nobody should seek his own good, but the good of others." 1 Corinthians 10:23-24

According to Mothers Against Drunk Driving (MADD), "In 2015, 10,265 people died in drunk driving crashes—one every 51 minutes—and 290,000 were injured in drunk driving crashes."[12] One of the 10,265 people killed that year was my amazing dad. Also noteworthy is this statistic, **"An average drunk driver has driven drunk over 80 times before first arrest."**[13] Let that sink in for a moment.

These figures translate to many thousands of impaired drivers on the roads at any given time of day or night. My dad was hit at 1:30 on a clear, sunny Monday

---

[12] https://www.madd.org/statistics/
[13] Ibid

afternoon. It wasn't a holiday or a weekend or a special occasion or bad weather, just a regular weekday afternoon when he wouldn't have dreamed that he would be in danger from an impaired driver. *One never knows.*

This is the DUI Memorial Sign that the Georgia Department of Transportation placed for my dad at the crash site.

This chapter might be your least favorite in the book. I understand that many people drink alcohol—the majority of the people I know are drinkers to some degree, and with the legalization of marijuana in a growing number of states, smoking marijuana and other drug use and abuse is on the rise. I certainly don't mean to offend anyone or step on toes; I simply want to bring out some points for consideration, so I urge you to stick with me.

I have always hated alcohol. I'm not really sure why, but even as a young child, I felt very uncomfortable around people who were drinking.

In high school, I was one of the founding members of the Students Against Drunk Driving (SADD) club. At the honors day program the last week of my senior year, I was presented with a very special award and scholarship. The mother of a young man who had been killed by a drunk driver in the county where my dad was raised presented me with a $300 scholarship check because of my involvement in the SADD club. Though I was thankful for the recognition and the scholarship, I had no idea how my life would be impacted years later by an intoxicated driver, also.

I recently saw the younger sister of that young man who had lost his life to a drunk driver, and I commented to her how ironic it was that I had received the scholarship in honor of her brother, and now we're dealing with my dad's loss as a result of DUI as well.

The negative feelings I had about alcohol only increased as my dad began his career in counseling and would come home to share snippets about people whose lives were in shambles because of alcohol and drug use and abuse. I vowed never to drink (or do drugs, of course), and I vowed not to marry anyone who did so, either.

Some studies have shown that certain people are "predisposed" to substance addiction. My opinion is that it's more spiritual than anything, however, because patterns of sin can be carried on from generation to generation unless the chain is broken. Certainly there's an element of environment involved as well because if someone grows up in an alcoholic household (or with an alcoholic grandparent), he or she has learned those addictive patterns and behaviors first hand.

However, drinking alcohol or taking drugs is completely and totally voluntary—a choice. Some people call substance addiction a disease, but it's unlike any other disease I can fathom. It's non-communicable, and it's one hundred percent preventable. Yes, substance addiction destroys lives and families, but in my mind, comparing addiction to diseases like cancer or diabetes or asthma or Alzheimer's is unfair. Because one doesn't know whether he or she might have a tendency to have a problem with such substances, it's best never to try them in the first place.

Another argument against alcohol consumption is that you might not have a problem with alcohol, but your children might grow up and have a problem with it. Could you live with yourself if they learned to drink from you and they went on to kill someone or ruin their own lives with addiction? I've heard horror stories of this happening. What about others on whom you have influence? Remember that if we profess Christ, the world is always watching us. "It is better not to eat meat or drink wine or to do anything else that will cause your brother to fall." Romans 15:16

My two older sons are high schoolers but are taking college classes through our state's dual enrollment program, which means they are taking college classes that give them high school and college credit at the same time. Interestingly, as I was getting ready to publish this book, my boys received a lengthy email from one of their colleges detailing concerns about the growing pattern of alcohol and drug abuse and what the college is doing to reduce this usage and to educate students and staff about the dangers associated with using such substances.

The email said, "Many well-documented risks are associated with alcohol and other drugs, affecting not only the individual user but also the user's family, friends and communities. Alcohol is frequently implicated in cases of sexual misconduct on campus, for example, and the misuse of other drugs is sometimes a factor in other violent behavior. Problems associated with alcohol and other drugs include impaired brain function; poor academic or job performance; relationship difficulties, including sexual dysfunction; a tendency to verbal and physical violence; financial distress; injuries or accidents; violations of the law such as driving under the influence; willfully destroying property; and death." [14]

After detailing the risks associated with use and abuse of alcohol and other drugs and then describing the college and criminal sanctions regarding these activities, the email provided a list of sources for help with alcohol and drug dependency. Substance abuse is a major problem in our society.

Here's something to try. Make a list of all of the ways that drinking or using drugs

---

[14] Email communication from Lanier Technical College. Gainesville, GA. Retrieved April 24, 2019.

might benefit you. Then make a list of all of the ways that those behaviors can harm you or others. I think you'll read a lopsided list. I can think of zero benefits of consuming alcohol. Some might claim that it helps them to relax. I would argue that God can do the same thing as we bring our anxieties to Him in prayer. Anything that takes us away from our dependence on God should be avoided.

There have been a number of times through my years of parenting small children that I jokingly said to my husband or my sister or my parents, "I need a drink." That was funny then because they knew that I would never actually partake, but some situations in life made me wish that I could escape in one form or another. I understand the temptation of drinking something that has the potential to make one feel better about whatever is happening in life—to take away the stress or pain.

But here's the problem: The stressful situation wouldn't have changed if I had ingested an alcoholic beverage. I would've simply dulled my senses in an attempt to mask the pain or ease the tension in my life. What would I have taught my children? That when things get tough, we turn to a drug to make us feel better instead of to our loving Heavenly Father, who has promised to carry us through every difficult situation in this life.

If one person reading this book decides not to drink again, and as a result, one person's life is saved, all of my efforts will be worth it. We might never know this side of eternity how things might've turned out if we had made different choices, but I trust that the Lord will bless our efforts as we do what He leads us to do.

"Do not get drunk on wine, which leads to debauchery. Instead, be filled with the Spirit." Ephesians 5:18

"But the fruit of the Spirit is love, joy, peace, patience, kindness, goodness, faithfulness, gentleness, and self-control. Against such things there is no law." Galatians 5:22-23

Chapter 7: "Firsts" and Anniversaries

"When you pass through the waters, I will be with you; and when you pass through the rivers, they will not sweep over you. When you walk through the fire, you will not be burned; the flames will not set you ablaze." Isaiah 43:2

In the hours and days following the crash, I received a flurry of comforting Facebook messages, texts, emails, cards, and calls from friends. I appreciated all of them, but one in particular from my friend and cousin, Kasi, has stuck with me. She lost her mother to cancer a few years before my dad was killed, so she understood the heartache of losing a parent who was also a dear friend.

She wrote, "I know that sickening ache that is indescribable and I am so very sorry you are experiencing it. I have found that the hardest times for me aren't the ones I already expect to be hard....the "firsts"....1st Christmas without them, 1st birthday, 1st Mother's/Father's Day, etc. It's the times when I'm least expecting it....driving down the road and think of her or have the impulse to call her, then realize I can't. Those times aren't expected and will slap you square in the face.

"The hardest of all, though, is when my girls say they miss her. It's almost unbearable. I get mad at what they are missing out on by having her as a grandmother. I say all of this not to make a bad situation worse, but to warn you to brace yourself when you can because I know how close you were/are to your parents and how close your parents are to your children. It's hard enough for adults to process, but I feel so deeply for your children who are robbed of their grandfather.

"Don't be afraid to cry out to Him! Remember, even Jesus did it on the cross. Looking back, I know there is no way I could have made it through many days with my own strength. I give credit to God for carrying me when I've been too weak on my own. Lifting you up until we talk again soon. Much love!!"

Kasi was exactly right. I've found that some of those moments that occur out of the blue have thrown me for a loop—the desire to call him and then remembering that I can't; going through his office at church and finding an empty Starbucks cup (he loved Starbucks coffee); receiving the gift of a bracelet with his handwriting engraved on it; or hearing a song from his funeral on the radio. I try to maintain my composure most of the time, but those are the moments that knock the breath out of me.

Some of the "firsts," the anniversaries that we all dreaded, have been harder than others. Dad was killed in May, 2015. The next month, we had three "firsts." Mom and Dad's anniversary was June 7, Dad's birthday was June 9, and Father's Day was June 16. I wanted to crawl in a hole and stay there the entire month. Our pain was so raw that we just did what we could to survive those first few weeks.

As the months after the crash went by, we began to have some discussions about things that we could do to celebrate Dad and bring some meaning to other "firsts." Looking back, those events were more bearable because of some of the things that we did to prepare for them. Let me explain.

My dad was a huge University of Georgia football fan. For our first Christmas without him, my mom got a small "Papa" tree for her living room and decorated it with UGA-themed ornaments. The bow on his casket was made from red UGA ribbon, so we attached that bow to the top of the tree as the topper. I ordered some photo ornaments for the tree with pictures of Dad with each of us. It gave us a visible reminder of him and helped us to celebrate who he was.

Our "Papa" Christmas tree

Also that first Christmas, we gave all of
our family a piece of jewelry made from
dried, crushed flowers from Dad's funeral.
We gave Dad's mom and sisters a bracelet,
and all of the guys received a cross
bookmark. It was truly meaningful, and it

helped us to focus on others instead of our own pain.

The next Christmas, my sister gave Mom and me silver bracelets that had Dad's handwriting engraved on them. Mine says,

I love you

Dad

I wear the bracelet almost every day, and I can always look down and see my dad's very distinctive handwriting telling me that he loves me. On my other arm, I wear a bracelet from my sweet friend, Elizabeth, with a paraphrase of Romans 8:28 on it. It says, "He works all things together for our good." These are constant reminders that my Heavenly Father knows my pain, loves me through it, and will make all things right one day.

I deeply dreaded the first anniversary of the crash. I was nauseated every time it came to mind. As my mom and sister and I discussed the approaching date, we wanted to do something that would celebrate Dad's life and who he was while on this earth. Dad was all about giving. For years and years, the church that he pastored took bags filled with household essentials to a local housing project every month. He led multiple similar servant evangelism projects through the years—giving away 9-volt batteries for smoke alarms, water bottles during the local fall festivals, Hershey kisses for Valentine's Day, and carnations for Mothers' Day. He went on numerous mission trips to Peru. He took the instruction of Jesus to share the Gospel and minister to the poor very seriously. He was generous with his time and his resources.

Ultimately, what we decided to do to commemorate the first anniversary of Dad's death was to take lunch to all of the first responders who worked the scene of the crash when Dad was killed. We ordered barbeque and pizza and delivered it to the Georgia State Patrol office, the Braselton Police Department, and the Braselton fire station.

Our visit to thank and encourage the Specialized Collision Reconstruction Team at the Georgia State Patrol post.

We told the first responders and the investigators how much they meant to us and how thankful we are for them and their compassion, and we prayed for them. We understand that they deal with horrific scenes day in and day out. The trauma that they encounter regularly would leave me in a lump of tears. I can't imagine how they cope with the heaviness of death and destruction and then show the care and compassion that our family received. They need our prayers on a regular basis.

If you have "firsts" approaching, or other anniversaries, I encourage you to find ways to make them meaningful. Focus on serving others. It's not that we ignore our own pain on those days—the pain is always there, but in the process of serving, the Lord seems to pour out His healing balm on our own sorrowful hearts in greater measure.

Chapter 8: Dreams

"In the last days, God says, I will pour out my Spirit on all people. Your sons and daughters will prophesy, your young men will see visions, your old men will dream dreams." Acts 2:17

In the Bible, dreams were very important. God sometimes communicated with His people in dreams about events that were to come. Dreams brought comfort or warnings to God's people, and God sometimes used them to give instruction. In Genesis, Joseph had dreams about his brothers bowing down to him, and later he was able to interpret dreams that his fellow prisoners had. The Bible tells us that "Daniel could understand visions and dreams of all kinds." (Daniel 1:17)

Even the earthly father of Jesus—Joseph—was instructed in a dream to take Mary to be his wife. He later had a dream warning him to flee to Egypt: "an angel of the Lord appeared to Joseph in a dream.

'Get up,' he said, 'take the child and his mother and escape to Egypt. Stay there until I tell you, for Herod is going to search for the child to kill him.'" (Matthew 2:13)

I have a friend whose dad died suddenly many years ago. It was Christmas time, and she was out shopping for gifts. She returned home to find that her dad had had a massive heart attack and died. There was no chance to say goodbye or any of the things that we want to say to our loved ones before they leave this world.

For two years, my friend prayed for dreams of her dad. Then finally one night, she had a very vivid vision of her dad. He was at the foot of her bed, holding a gift. He told her that a church friend was in the hospital, which turned out to be true. It was a precious encounter, and it gave my friend peace about her dad.

After Dad was killed, my mom, sister, and I desperately wanted to see him and talk to him in our dreams. I imagine this is a normal desire, to spend time again with a loved one who is deceased, if only in our subconscious. I believe that God still speaks to us in our dreams. I don't pretend to be an expert on interpretation of dreams, but I believe that there is something meaningful in the dreams that we have had about my dad.

I first dreamed about Dad a few months after he was killed. In my dream, I was talking to him on the phone. He was in Heaven; I was here on earth. We were carrying on a conversation much like we did when he was alive. I was asking him what it's like there in Heaven. I didn't see him, but it was comforting to talk to him and know that he was okay.

Some months later, I had another dream. This one was disturbing in a sense, but it made me thankful, too. I'll describe it momentarily, but first a little background.

After the crash that killed my dad, I had a strange hope that the crime lab that was doing the autopsy would find a terrible disease or evidence that he would've died a horrible death, had he not been killed. I wanted his tragic death to turn out to be merciful, sparing him awful suffering from cancer or some other wasting disease. We never heard that any such evidence was found in the autopsy.

In my second dream, my dad had cancer. He was in terrible pain and was suffering immensely. My sister also dreamed that Dad had cancer and was wasting away from the horrible disease.

My mom later dreamed that Dad had survived the crash, but his body was broken and battered. He was somewhat ambulatory in her dream, but as he was walking around one day with much effort and pain, he suddenly lay down on the couch and died.

In all three of our dreams, God showed us how things might have been. It was as if the Lord was telling us that the manner of Dad's death was, indeed, His mercy.

If you long to see your loved one in dreams, ask God to give those dreams to you. As you lay your head on your pillow at night, ask The Father if He will bless you with dreams and visions of your dad or mom or spouse or sibling or child or friend that you miss so very much. It took many months of asking God for dreams of Dad before I actually had one, so be persistent. He loves to bless us, and He knows what will comfort our hurting hearts.

When you have those dreams, ask God to show you what they mean. God often speaks to us in our dreams. Perhaps he's simply comforting you, or maybe he wants to direct you to some action, but be open as you pray for interpretation, and trust that He has your best interests at heart. Also, be sure to write down your dreams because the memory of them fades over time, and that is something that you want to be certain to remember always.

Sweet dreams, friends.

Chapter 9: Pets

"Are not five sparrows sold for two pennies? Yet not one of them is forgotten by God." Luke 12:6

This might sound unbelievable, but before the crash, our four kids had never had a furry pet. I had always denied my children's requests for dogs or cats, explaining, "We have four children; we don't need pets." I had my hands more than full with homeschooling and caring for four kids full time, so I never wanted the responsibility and work that I knew pets would bring.

We did get the kids some goldfish and betta fish a few years back, and my middle son caught a crawdad near our home that we kept for a couple of years. He was affectionately named "Craw Man." But even then, almost all of the care and maintenance for the animals fell into my lap.

That's why, when just months after the crash, I really surprised myself when I agreed to the kids' request for a kitten. We visited a local pet store on their Humane Society Adoption Day and adopted a beautiful orange kitten whom we named Tigger. He was around five months old when we adopted him, and he has grown into a fat, lazy cat who loves to play outside and come in occasionally to eat and sleep.

Me with Tigger on the day that we adopted him.

Though we adore Tigger, he doesn't often return the affection. He very rarely lets us pet him, slinking his back down if we even try. If he is very sleepy, he will endure some loving strokes, but otherwise, it's mostly hands off.

So a few months after we adopted Tigger, the kids started asking for another kitten. They argued that it might be good for Tigger to have a playmate, and in my desire to have an affectionate and loving pet, I helped them approach Daddy with the idea. Though not crazy about the idea of having two cats, he went along with it.

The kids and I visited our local Humane Society right before Thanksgiving and spent a long while in the cat room. We took out several kittens, holding them and observing how they interacted with other cats. Upon the advice of the employee who was helping us, we settled on an interesting-looking female kitten whom we named Sassy. Sassy is mostly gray, but she has orange stripes on her back legs, with white feet and a white tummy.

The Lord was certainly in our decision, because Sassy was the perfect addition to our family. She and Tigger have become the best of friends. They wrestle and chase each other around. Then when they get tired, they curl up and nap side by side. Sassy is playful and energetic, yet she loves to crawl into our laps to cuddle.

According to *The Catnip Times*, "Animals offer many perks to our happiness by increasing oxytocin, dopamine, serotonin, *and* endorphins in our brains, leaving us feeling happier whenever we are around them. For those dealing with the effects of grief, these feelings can be extremely important in helping to cope."

The article continues, "The great thing about a cat's [or dog's] companionship is the absence of expectation. Sometimes it can be hard to experience companionship with people in times of grief in a way that isn't overwhelming to the process. With an animal's companionship comes a no-nonsense relationship that can help mental health and feelings of loneliness without leaving a person feeling like they have to say a certain thing, act a certain way, or interact in socially expectant ways. Seeking face-to-face support can be a healthy step in coping with grief, but support offered by an animal that doesn't require the same expectations that human interaction does can be helpful as well."[15]

I know that pets are used in therapy with Alzheimer's patients and in nursing home settings, but I'm now convinced that the Lord uses pets as a salve in other hurtful situations as well. Our pets have brought us laughter and affection, have helped us to teach the children about responsibility and caring for others, and have been a soothing balm for our souls.

Even my husband, who has never been an animal person, has quite an affection for our furry friends. It's heartwarming to see and experience. If your family doesn't have a pet, you might consider whether adopting one would work with your schedule and your financial situation. Not

---

[15] https://www.thecatniptimes.com/learn/cat-behavior/how-cats-help-us-cope-with-grief/

everyone enjoys animals, but for those who do, they can be a source of much comfort and joy.

Chapter 10: Music "Therapy"

"As the deer pants for streams of water, so my soul pants for you, O God." Psalm 42:1

I don't know about you, but the Lord often uses music to minister to me or speak to me. We were created as musical beings. We were made to worship Him through song. There is an entire book of songs included in Scripture (Psalms), so God obviously thinks that music is important for us. God often uses music to reach our spirits at a level that words simply can't touch.

According to the American Music Therapy Association, "Music Therapy is an established health profession in which music is used within a therapeutic relationship to address physical, emotional, cognitive, and social needs of individuals. After assessing the strengths and needs of each client, the qualified music therapist provides the indicated treatment including creating, singing, moving to, and/or listening to music. Through musical involvement in the therapeutic context, clients' abilities are strengthened and transferred to other areas of their lives. Music therapy also provides avenues for communication that can be helpful to those who find it difficult to express themselves in words. Research in music therapy supports its effectiveness in many areas such as: overall physical rehabilitation and facilitating movement, increasing people's motivation to become engaged in their treatment, providing emotional support for clients and their families, and providing an outlet for expression of feelings." [16]

Lois Chapman Dick says in *Living with Grief after Sudden Loss* that, "For some people one of the best physical exercises to relieve stress/trauma can be

---

[16]

https://www.musictherapy.org/about/musictherapy

dancing/bouncing/marching to music they love." [17]

After Dad was killed, certain songs were especially impactful in my life. I would listen to them over and over and shed many healing tears of sorrow. Some songs talk about the goodness of God in spite of our pain; others focus more on the fact that this world isn't our home and we are destined for a much better place.

If you find comfort in music also, I encourage you to read the following lyrics several times and let the Lord pour His healing balm over your spirit. Then find the songs on YouTube and listen to Him speak to you through them.

Shortly after the crash, I made a new play list on my phone music app called "Papa," and I loaded songs there that ministered to me during that time. There are times when some of the songs are too painful to listen

---

[17] Dick, Lois C. "Impact on Enforcement and EMS Personnel." *Living with Grief after Sudden Loss*. Washington: The Hospice Foundation of America. 1996. Page 183. Print.

to; other times they are just what I need to hear.

Here are a few that I want to share with you. There are many others that are meaningful and powerful. I hope you will allow the Lord to speak to you through music, as well.

The first song that I want to share is "I Am Not Alone" by Kari Jobe. It was one that I listened to many times right after Dad was killed. I could especially relate to the lyrics, as I certainly felt like I was walking "through deep waters" in "the midst of deep sorrow" at the time. The song is so meaningful that I titled this book, *Through Deep Waters*, after the first line.

I love what Kari Jobe said about her song, "There are so many hard things we face on this side of heaven. Songs that minister to me the most are ones that remind me God knows and sees where I am and is working on my behalf. It's real and it's life. What a sweet reminder that we are not alone and that we have a mighty God who

goes before us, and never ever leaves us.
This song inspires us to 'draw near to God
and He will draw near to us' (James
4:8)."[18]

"I Am Not Alone" by Kari Jobe

"When I walk through deep waters
I know that You will be with me
When I'm standing in the fire
I will not be overcome
Through the valley of the shadow
I will not fear

I am not alone
I am not alone
You will go before me
You will never leave me

In the midst of deep sorrow
I see Your light is breaking through
The dark of night will not overtake me
I am pressing into You
Lord, You fight my every battle
And I will not fear

---

[18] https://praisecleveland.com/1972920/kari-jobe-
explains-story-behind-i-am-not-alone/

You amaze me
Redeem me
You call me as Your own"[19]

Next is "I Have This Hope" by Tenth
Avenue North. This one assured me over
and over, when "my faith felt thin and I
thought the night would never end," that
my hope is in the Lord. He is with me and
will never let me go.

"I Have This Hope" by Tenth Avenue North

"As I walk this great unknown
Questions come and questions go
Was there purpose for the pain?
Did I cry these tears in vain?

I don't want to live in fear
I want to trust that You are near
Trust Your grace can be seen
In both triumph and tragedy

I have this hope
In the depth of my soul

---

[19]

https://www.azlyrics.com/lyrics/karijobe/iamnotalo
ne.html

In the flood or the fire
You're with me and You won't let go

But sometimes my faith feels thin
Like the night will never end
Will You catch every tear
Or will You just leave me here?

But I have this hope
In the depth of my soul
In the flood or the fire
You're with me and You won't let go

Yes, I have this hope
In the depth of my soul
In the flood or the fire
You're with me and You won't let go

So, whatever happens I will not be afraid
Cause You are closer than this breath that
I take
You calm the storm when I hear You call
my name
I still believe that one day I'll see Your
face

I have this hope
In the depth of my soul

In the flood or the fire
You're with me

I have this hope
In the depth of my soul
In the flood or the fire
You're with me and You won't let go

In the flood or the fire
You're with me and You won't let go

In the flood or the fire
You're with me and You won't let go"[20]

Next is "Where I Belong" by Building 429. This one was so reassuring because I knew that the intense pain that I was feeling was not going to be with me forever. This world is not my home, and all will be made right soon and very soon.

"Where I Belong" by Building 429

"Sometimes it feels like I'm watching from
the outside
Sometimes it feels like I'm breathing, but

---

[20]
https://www.azlyrics.com/lyrics/tenthavenuenorth/i havethishope.html

am I alive?
I will keep searching for answers that
aren't here to find

All I know is I'm not home yet
This is not where I belong
Take this world and give me Jesus
This is not where I belong

So when the walls come falling down on
me
And when I'm lost in the current of a
raging sea
I have this blessed assurance holding me

All I know is I'm not home yet
This is not where I belong
Take this world and give me Jesus
This is not where I belong

When the earth shakes
I wanna be found in you
When the lights fade
I wanna be found in you

All I know is I'm not home yet
This is not where I belong
Take this world and give me Jesus
This is not where I belong

All I know is I'm not home yet
This is not where I belong
Take this world and give me Jesus
This is not where I belong

Where I belong
where I belong
Where I belong
where I belong"[21]

The last song that I want to share with you is "King of My Heart" by Kutlass. I first heard this song at a ladies' retreat that I attended with my friend Elizabeth shortly after Dad was killed. It was so painful that first time I heard it. I couldn't bring myself to sing along, because how could God be good if He allowed me to hurt so much? I felt like He *had* let me down.

In the years since then, I have sung this song many times, and I believe that as I sing the words, I am affirming the goodness of God, even when I don't feel it. In other words, I speak what I know in my head to be true, and I trust that my

---

[21] https://www.azlyrics.com/lyrics/building429/whereibelonglive.html

feelings will catch up. God *is* good, and
He will *never* let me down.

"King of My Heart" by Kutlass

Let the King of my heart
Be the mountain where I run
The fountain I drink from
Oh He is my Song

Let the King of my heart
Be the shadow where I hide
The ransom for my life
Oh He is my Song

You are good, good, oh
You are good, good, oh
You are good, good, oh
You are good, good, oh

Let the King of my heart
Be the wind inside my sails
The anchor in the waves
Oh He is my Song

Let the King of my heart
Be the fire inside my veins
The echo of my days
Oh He is my Song

You are good, good, oh
You are good, good, oh
Yes, you are good, good, oh
You are good, good, oh

You're never gonna let, never gonna let
me down
You're never gonna let, never gonna let
me down
You're never gonna let, never gonna let
me down
You're never gonna let, never gonna let
me down

You are good, good, oh
You are good, good, oh
You are good, good, oh
You are good, good, oh
When the night is holding on to me
You are holding on

When the night is holding on to me
You are holding on
You are good, good, oh
You are good, good, oh
You are good, good, oh
You are good, good, oh

When the night is holding on to me
God is holding on

When the night is holding on to me
God is holding on [22]

---

[22]

https://www.azlyrics.com/lyrics/kutless/kingofmyhe
art.html

Chapter 11: Don't Hesitate

"'For I know the plans I have for you,'" declares the LORD, 'plans to prosper you and not to harm you, plans to give you hope and a future.'" Jeremiah 29:11

When my husband and I were planning our wedding, we struggled a little with what church we would plug into once we were married. Trevor had grown up in and was still attending a traditional Southern Baptist church. I was involved with a contemporary Vineyard church. We both loved our churches and worship styles, so we needed to find a church that would be a good compromise. We chose a Southern Baptist church that had contemporary worship music and solid, biblical teaching. It was just what we needed. We grew there, made some life-long friends, and had opportunities to pour out, too, by leading some Bible studies about finances.

Three years into our marriage, my dad, a local Vineyard pastor, met with us and asked if we would pray about coming to lead the youth group at his church. We decided that God was leading us in that direction, so in 2000, we became a part of The Gainesville Vineyard Christian Fellowship. Once our own children started coming along, however, we passed the youth group on to others and have ministered in various other ways. Our kids have been blessed to grow up in my parents' church, with Papa as their pastor.

Trevor and I have four children (plus one in Heaven). Our oldest is Caleb, born in 2002. He is the oldest of my parents' eleven grandchildren. On April 19, 2015, the Sunday before Caleb's thirteenth birthday, my dad called Caleb in front of the church to pray a blessing over him—not only a pastor's blessing but a grandfather's blessing. Trevor stood with them and prayed a father's blessing over Caleb as well.

As they were praying, I felt a prompting to capture the moment by taking this picture with my phone. I'm so glad I did.

My dad and my husband Trevor praying over our oldest son as he was turning 13.

As you know, two weeks later, on May 4, my dad was killed in a hit-and-run crash by an intoxicated driver while cycling near his home. I will always treasure this picture and the memory of what Dad did for Caleb. I made a print of it and framed it for Caleb's room. Dad felt God leading him to acknowledge Caleb's transition into manhood by praying over him. I'm so thankful that he didn't *hesitate*.

We face situations every day in which we might feel a gentle nudge in our spirits to do something that would minister to others. Maybe the grumpy cashier at the grocery store, who is obviously having a bad day (or a bad life), could use a word of encouragement. Perhaps the person behind us in the drive-thru line would appreciate our paying for his meal. Or maybe we should take a moment to write a note to, or better yet, visit an older person who struggles with loneliness.

There are countless ways that God prompts us to reach out to those who need a touch from Him, even in the midst of our own pain and brokenness. We are the hands and feet of Jesus on this earth, so God uses us to accomplish His purposes here. Do we listen for the still, small voice of the Holy Spirit leading us as we go about our business, or are we too busy and distracted to look outward to the needs of others? When we do sense God leading us to step out, do we hesitate or do we obey?

I'm certainly guilty of hesitating or of missing the moment because I'm too inward focused at times. It takes effort to reach out to others when life is already hard and full. I wonder how many times I have missed the blessing of being used by God because I was consumed by what was going on in my own life and circumstances and didn't obey His direction.

Here are some verses that might help us to be more intentional about ministering to others as we go about our business each day:

"But I tell you who hear me: Love your enemies, do good to those who hate you, bless those who curse you, pray for those who mistreat you." Luke 6:27-28

"Never be lacking in zeal, but keep your spiritual fervor, serving the Lord." Romans 12:11

"Do not merely listen to the word, and so deceive yourselves. Do what it says." James 1:22

"Those who are led by the Spirit of God are sons of God." Romans 8:14

"My command is this: love each other as I have loved you. Greater love has no one than this, that he lay down his life for his friends." John 15:12-13

"A generous man will prosper; he who refreshes others will himself be refreshed." Proverbs 11:25

Let's be intentional about obeying the promptings of the Lord without hesitation, so that we can help to bring about His Kingdom here on earth. I don't know about you, but I'm ready for Jesus to return for His Church. I believe the more we help accomplish His purposes here, the sooner He will come for us.

Come, Lord Jesus!

Chapter 12: Dads, Write Notes to Your Children

"Fix these words of mine in your hearts and minds; tie them as symbols on your hands and bind them on your foreheads. Teach them to your children, talking about them when you sit at home and when you walk along the road, when you lie down and when you get up." Deuteronomy 11:18-19

I would like to take a few moments to encourage you to do something that will mean the world to your children and maybe even your grandchildren one day. This isn't a hard task, and it will take very little planning and effort. This chapter isn't really about help with your grieving process, but it might be comforting to know that you are being intentional about leaving a legacy of love and encouragement and blessing for future generations.

I was a student at North Georgia College in beautiful Dahlonega, Georgia, in the mid-1990s. The campus was about an hour's drive from my parents' home. Because my grandparents lived about half as far from school, I stayed with them during the school week, to make my commute shorter and cheaper. Then I went home on the weekends.

One day after class, I got to my car to head back to my grandparents' house and found a note from my dad, scribbled on the back of his business card and slid under my windshield wiper. He was a licensed professional counselor and was working that day making home visits in the area where my college was located.

Here's the note:

Michelle Fitzpatrick Thomas

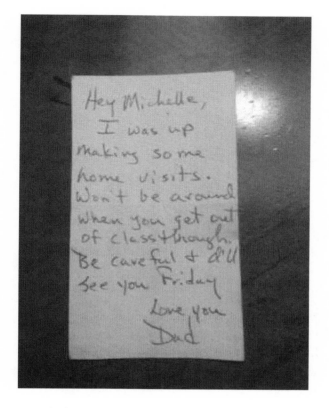

My dad had taken time out of his schedule that day to weave through the large college parking lots and locate my car so he could let me know that he was thinking of me and loved me.

It has been *many* years since I found the note on my car, and I have kept it secure

143

in the bottom drawer of my jewelry box ever since. In other words, I have *treasured* it.

After my dad was killed, I searched through boxes and containers of stuff that we have stored in closets and behind knee walls. I was desperate for more written notes from my dad, specifically to me, telling me that he loves me. I found a couple of cards that he wrote to my husband and me early in our marriage, thanking us for contributing to his mission trips to Peru. He also wrote the inscription on a Bible that he and my mom gave me for Christmas one year.

I hope there are other notes from my dad that I have yet to find, but most of the birthday cards and inscriptions and notes and such were written by my mom. Of course, I treasure those also, but like all daddy's girls, this one craves written affirmation and encouragement and love from her daddy.

My encouragement to dads today is to be intentional about writing notes to your

children. Write on their birthday cards
some of the time. Scribble an "I love you"
on the napkin in their lunchbox. Keep a
journal for each child, and write to them in
it occasionally, telling them how special
they are and what you enjoy about them—
something my husband and I have been
doing since our children were born. Then
present it to them when they are grown
and ready to leave your nest.

If your children are already grown, mail
them a "Thinking of You" card and tell
them how proud you are of them and how
much you love them. Those little
intentional acts of love might mean the
world to your children one day.

I realize that these sentimental kinds of
things come naturally to moms and not so
much to most dads. I know that life is
busy and it's easy to forego the little
extras, but please take a few moments
occasionally to write special things to your
kids. Life is a vapor, and we never know if
we will have tomorrow.

Thankfully, our Heavenly Daddy wrote many amazing love notes to us in His Word, The Bible, and we can draw comfort and strength from them always.

Here are some of my favorites:

"The Lord your God is with you, He is mighty to save. He will take great delight in you, He will quiet you with His love, He will rejoice over you with singing." (Zephaniah 3:17)

"I have loved you with an everlasting love. I have drawn you with loving-kindness." (Jeremiah 31:3)

"For God so loved the world that He gave His one and only Son, that whoever believes in Him shall not perish but have eternal life." (John 3:16)

Amen

Chapter 13: A Journey Through Grief, A Promise of Hope

"May the God of hope fill you with all joy and peace as you trust in him, so that you may overflow with hope by the power of the Holy Spirit." Romans 15:13

My sister Suzanne is a very talented writer. She wrote a precious poem for my wedding day and presented it to me written in beautiful calligraphy and framed. I will always treasure it. As I mentioned, she's an RN and lactation consultant. As an aside, she is writing a marvelous book about breastfeeding called *The Breastfeeding Mom's Survival Guide: Surviving and Thriving Through the First Two Weeks and Beyond.* It should be available sometime in 2019. If you are in that season of life or if you have a loved one who needs help and encouragement in the area of breastfeeding, I encourage you to check out her book.

Suzanne penned the following poem for the first anniversary of our dad's death. I want to share it with you, and I hope that it touches your heart as much as it did mine. It is truly a picture of how much our Heavenly Father adores us and desires close relationship with us.

A Journey Through Grief, A Promise of Hope

by Suzanne Fitzpatrick Nunnally

May 4, 2016

A beautiful Monday in the heart of spring,

Such peace in my heart, full of thanksgiving.

I told the Lord, "Life is perfect, please let it stay."

No idea what would be changed by the end of the day.

Through random circumstances we had a
clue

That something was wrong; in our hearts
we knew.

And at the scene, it was confirmed to be
him.

My dad was gone, and this nightmare
begins.

The first few days pass by with a blur.

Friends and family surround you, give you
strength to endure.

I want to wake up from this nightmare, I
say.

It can't be true, I will wake up some day.

But each day, each moment, the truth hits
again,

My dad, my greatest friend, is gone to
Heaven.

And so this journey with grief, it starts to take hold

The loss and the pain will lessen we're told.

I want time to stop, but move fast just the same.

I long for a time when I can breathe again.

But the farther I go, the longer it's been

Since I saw him, hugged him, breathed him in.

The world keeps on moving, as if all is the same,

But inside I scream "Stop!" I can't play this game.

Don't people know that I'm not okay?

That this pain and the grief don't just go away?

My faith starts to shake, I'm angry, it's
true.

I needed my dad, and I know God knew.

But just when my faith starts to break, I
can take no more,

God gives me a hope, like never before.

God promises always to work for our
good.

My mind can't contain what He
understood.

His plan is much bigger and broader than
mine.

He weaves it all together from the
beginning of time.

And yes, the hole in my life is great and
wide,

But God promises always to be by my
side.

I cried out to God, said I needed my dad.

He said, "I'm the best Dad you've ever had."

So hold me, my Daddy, please don't let go.

Walk with me through life, and I will know

That even through loss and sorrow and grief,

You love me, sustain me, secure my belief.

And even though joy is shadowed with pain.

Our loss on this Earth is Heaven's gain.

I rejoice in the promise I'll see him someday

When I'm fully alive in Heaven to stay.

Chapter 14: Heaven

"For here we do not have an enduring city, but we are looking for the city that is to come." Hebrews 13:14

As I mentioned previously, before my dad was killed, I had some fear of dying. I believe it's normal to have anxiety regarding the unknown. I knew that Heaven is perfect and that I wanted to go there when I died, but I was a bit apprehensive about leaving behind this world and the things that are comfortable to me.

After the crash, that all changed. In the months following Dad's death, I had an almost overwhelming desire to leave this world. Not in the sense that I was suicidal at all. I was simply ready to go whenever and as soon as the Lord would take me. I missed my dad so intensely, and there was such excruciating pain in my life on this earth; I knew that the pain would be gone once I was in Heaven.

My husband helped to bring me back to reality, as he often does, by reminding me how much I'm needed here and how horrible it would be for him and for my children if I were gone now. I knew that I had turned a corner when a few months after Dad's death, I had a strange pain in my abdomen. Fear suddenly gripped me with the thought that I might have cancer. I know that fear is not of the Lord, and it turned out to be nothing, but I no longer wanted to die right then and leave my babies here to grow up without me.

The reality is that unless Jesus returns for us soon, we all will die and leave this world, one way or another and at one time or another. Our job in the here and now is to serve the Lord faithfully and be ready whenever He chooses to bring us home to Him.

When I worked with Larry Burkett years ago, he used to say, "This earth is all the hell that Christians will ever experience, and it's the only Heaven that unbelievers will ever know." What a sobering thought. It's a joyful thought for Christians, because we are assured that we will leave behind the pain and sorrow and heartache that we experience here on earth to live forever with our loving Heavenly Father. But those who don't know the Lord as Savior will live in torment, separated from the Lord for eternity.

If you aren't sure of your relationship with the Lord, I plead with you to settle that right now. Jesus loves you. He came to earth as a human to live and die as the perfect sacrifice needed to atone for your sins and mine. All you have to do is repent of (turn your back on) your sins and receive the gift of salvation that He has made available to you. It is a decision that you will never regret. I will give you a money-back guarantee on that!

As I ponder Heaven now, I look forward with great anticipation to the day that I will join my dad and the host of other believers who have gone before me. I have been reading Randy Alcorn's book, *Heaven*, and it has been wonderful to see him unpack the Scriptures about what awaits us. I have such hope and such anticipation and such longing for my heavenly home.

Here are some Scriptures about Heaven that I hope will bring encouragement and comfort to your heart:

John 14:1-3:

"Do not let your hearts be troubled. Trust in God; trust also in me. In my Father's house are many rooms; if it were not so, I would have told you. I am going there to prepare a place for you. And if I go and prepare a place for you, I will come back and take you to be with me that you also may be where I am."

Revelation 21:3-8:

"And I heard a loud voice from the throne saying, 'Now the dwelling of God is with men, and he will live with them. They will be his people, and God himself will be with them and be their God. He will wipe every tear from their eyes. There will be no more death or mourning or crying or pain, for the old order of things has passed away.'

"He who was seated on the throne said, 'I am making everything new!' Then he said, 'Write this down, for these words are trustworthy and true.'

"He said to me: 'It is done. I am the Alpha and the Omega, the Beginning and the End. To him who is thirsty I will give to drink without cost from the spring of the water of life. He who overcomes will inherit all this, and I will be his God and he will be my son.'"

Revelation 7:13-17:

"Then one of the elders asked me, 'These in white robes—who are they, and where did they come from?'

"I answered, 'Sir, you know.'

"And he said, 'These are they who have come out of the great tribulation; they have washed their robes and made them white in the blood of the Lamb. Therefore, 'they are before the throne of God and serve him day and night in his temple; and he who sits on the throne will spread his tent over them. Never again will they hunger; never again will they thirst. The sun will not beat upon them, nor any scorching heat. For the Lamb at the center of the throne will be their shepherd; he will lead them to springs of living water. And God will wipe away every tear from their eyes.'"

Revelation 22:3-5:

"No longer will there be any curse. The throne of God and of the Lamb will be in the city, and his servants will serve him. They will see his face, and his name will be on their foreheads. There will be no more night. They will not need the light of a lamp or the light of the sun, for the Lord God will give them light. And they will reign for ever and ever."

Chapter 15: Helpful Resources

"Blessed are those who mourn, for they will be comforted." Matthew 5:4

Shortly after the crash that killed my dad, I emailed Focus on the Family. They sent me a list of resources that they recommend for people dealing with grief and loss. I ordered several of the books that were listed, and I want to share those with you, along with some other resources that our family has found to be helpful.

A Grace Disguised: How the Soul Grows Through Loss by Jerry Sittser, who lost his young daughter, his wife, and his mother in a DUI crash.

Choosing to See: A Journey of Struggle and Hope by Mary Beth Chapman. This is Steven Curtis Chapman's wife, writing about the loss of their daughter in an accident involving one of their sons.

Experiencing Grief by H. Norman Wright. This is a short and very helpful book about stages of grief and how to navigate them.

Forgiving the Unforgivable by Craig Stone. Several members of Stone's family were killed in a DUI crash. This is his story of working through the painful process of forgiving the driver.

Grace for the Widow: A Journey Through the Fog of Loss by Joyce Rogers. I haven't read this, but it has been encouraging to my mom.

Heaven by Randy Alcorn. This is a powerful reference book that helps us understand our eternal destination much better.

Hope for a Widow's Heart: Encouraging Reflections for your Journey by Quin Sherrer. I haven't read this, but my mom has found it helpful in her journey as a widow.

Living with Grief after Sudden Loss, edited by Kenneth J. Doka. This book was published by the Hospice Foundation of

America and is very helpful for people suffering sudden loss of any sort.

When Grief Comes: Finding Strength for Today and Hope for Tomorrow by Kirk H. Neely. Pastor Neely lost his son very unexpectedly and suddenly. His book is comforting.

You'll Get Through This: Hope and Help for your Turbulent Times by Max Lucado. This book is uplifting and encouraging for people going through all sorts of troubling times.

The full Focus on the Family resource list: http://media.focusonthefamily.com/topic info/grief_and_loss.pdf

Also, many churches host Grief Share support groups. For information about this opportunity and to look for groups in your area, visit GriefShare.org.

I also recommend that you allow your church to help you through this time. If you aren't in a small group already, this might be the time to join one. God puts us in communities so we can "carry each other's burdens, and in this way you will fulfill the law of Christ" (Galatians 6:2).

I hesitate to include this next tidbit, but it has been a game changer for me through this journey and it might really help some of you. I was 41 when my dad was killed. If you are a woman who is reading this book, you probably know that the 40s are a difficult time for us, hormonally. In the couple of years after Dad was killed, I really began to struggle with issues like anxiety, headaches, hot flashes, and just a general sense of feeling overwhelmed with life.

At the encouragement of my mom, I went to see a gynecologist who specializes in bioidentical hormone replacement therapy. I took a saliva hormone test, and it showed that my progesterone was almost off the bottom of the chart. She prescribed bioidentical hormones for me, and it has made a world of difference. Though I still struggle with anxiety sometimes, it is much milder and I am able to handle the stresses of life and the grief journey so much better. If you are struggling with these issues, I encourage you to find a doctor who will help you get your hormones straightened out.

Another thing to consider is that many people suffer from adrenal fatigue (hypoadrenia) during stressful times in their lives. "According to James Wilson, author of *Adrenal Fatigue: The 21st Century Stress Syndrome*, chronic stress and lifestyle affect the body's ability to recuperate from physical, mental or emotional stress."[23] There are natural supplements available at health food stores that can help restore your adrenals, enabling you to cope better with grief and life in general. There is a lot of information online regarding this issue, and many doctors of osteopathic medicine (DO) can give you guidance in this area as well.

One last bit of information: If you lost a loved one in the commission of a violent crime, you should be aware that all states have crime victim compensation programs

---

[23] https://draxe.com/3-steps-to-heal-adrenal-fatigue/

to help with your expenses. Here in
Georgia, the program helps pay for
medical and dental expenses, funeral
expenses, lost wages, counseling, and
crime scene sanitization.[24]

The program generally pays only if there
isn't other insurance or support available.
My mom was able to receive some help
with my dad's funeral expenses and lost
wages because the man who killed him
didn't have any insurance. For information
on your state's victim compensation
program, contact the district attorney's
office that is handling your loved one's
case.

[24] http://crimevictimscomp.ga.gov/for-victims/what-our-programs-cover/

Final Thoughts

I want to share some final thoughts with you as I close this book. As I was driving one day, the song by Chris Rice called "Untitled Hymn (Come to Jesus)" came on the radio. The last verse says, "With your final heartbeat, kiss the world goodbye. Then go in peace, and laugh on Glory's side. And Fly to Jesus. Fly to Jesus. Fly to Jesus and live."

I want you to know, friends, that when that truck hit my dad on May 4, 2015, he literally flew to Jesus. There was no warning. No time to prepare or say goodbye. One second he was enjoying a bike ride; the next he was in the arms of the Lord.

Thankfully, my dad was ready to enter eternity. He loved Jesus intensely and served Him unashamedly. He longed for his heavenly home as he was passing through this life. If your relationship with the Lord isn't what it should be, I plead with you to take care of that right now. He is waiting with open arms. We aren't promised tomorrow or this evening or even the next five seconds here on earth.

If you need help understanding the Christian life, a few great resources are Focus on the Family, Answers in Genesis, Samaritan's Purse, Ravi Zacharias, *World* magazine, SBC.net, VineyardUSA.org, and KLOVE.com.

As we all know, this world is hard and painful, but our God is good and loving and faithful. I will be with my Heavenly Father and with my dad again one day soon, and that assurance is what carries me. I hope you will join us there.

Blessings, friends.

Michelle

Made in the USA
Monee, IL
02 February 2020

21167607R00097